Profiles of Women

Past & Present

Profiles
of
Women

Past & Present

Fifteen Original
First Person Monologues
Written for Classroom
and Group Presentations

Created, Researched and Written by Members of the
Thousand Oaks California Branch Inc of
the American Association of University Women

VOLUME I

Illustrated by Ann Matthews

American Association of University Women
Thousand Oaks Branch Inc
California

To order additional copies, send a check for $9.95 each, plus
$2.50 shipping and handling (and California sales tax if
applicable) to: AAUW/Profiles, Thousand Oaks Branch,
Inc., P.O. Box 4223, Thousand Oaks, CA 91359-1223. Please
include your name, address, organization and/or school
district and phone number in all correspondence. Questions
and/or comments about your experiences with *Profiles of
Women, Past & Present* are encouraged and can be sent to the
above address.

The fifteen monologues in this book were researched, written, revised and
edited by past and/or current members of the Thousand Oaks, California
Branch, Inc. of the American Association of University Women. Although
every attempt has been made to verify the accuracy of these histories, this
has sometimes been difficult due to conflicting data or a lack of information regarding the sources originally consulted.

First Edition

Library of Congress Catalog Card Number 93-72554

ISBN 0-9637756-0-X

10 9 8 7 6 5 4 3 2 1

Printed in the U.S.A.

This book is dedicated to Sandy Hindy.
Her vision and dedication will encourage the girls and boys of today
to make career choices that are not bound by gender.

Acknowledgements

We would like to acknowledge the many friends, members and supporters of the Thousand Oaks, California Branch, Inc. of the American Association of University Women who helped us shape a dream into a reality:

Lawrence C. Janss and the School of the Pacific Islands who granted funds for publication;

Kate McLean and the Ventura County Community Foundation who facilitated the funding of the grant;

The many members of the Thousand Oaks, California Branch, Inc. of AAUW who conceived of the concept, researched, wrote, edited and adapted the monologues and presented these women to schools and groups throughout our community;

The Women's History Publication Committee who compiled, designed, edited and produced *Profiles of Women, Past & Present:* Joan Bennett, Amyra Braha, Colleen Briner-Schmidt, Ginny Cobb, Deborah Davis, Naomi Finkel, Louise Grethel, Pat Helton, Sandy Hindy, Donna Langley, Jill Lewis, Ricki Mikkelsen, Kathleen Sullivan, Deana Sun and Barbara Wilson;

And finally, the girls and boys in the classrooms who applauded our presentations and encouraged us in our endeavors.

Table of Contents

Introduction and History

Congratulations! You have purchased an exciting tool to bring women's history alive. *Profiles of Women, Past & Present* is a series of monologues which introduces the lives and achievements of women from past and present history. The fifteen monologues in this book were researched and written by members of the Thousand Oaks, California Branch, Inc. of the American Association of University Women (AAUW).

The idea for this book originated in 1985 when seven-year-old Stacey Hindy, the daughter of one of our branch members, broke her arm. At the doctor's, Stacey indicated that she could be a nurse when she grew up, but that "only men could be doctors." Her mother, Sandy, immediately saw a need to show her daughter, and other children, that women's aspirations need not be limited by gender stereotypes. She researched, wrote and then presented first person monologues highlighting the lives of women from history to students in grades one through six at her daughter's elementary school. One of the women she presented was Elizabeth Blackwell, America's first woman physician, demonstrating that girls could, indeed, be doctors.

The next year, the Thousand Oaks Branch of AAUW formed a committee to build on what Sandy had accomplished. Over sixty branch members became involved as researchers, writers, editors and presenters. During National Women's History Month in March 1987, AAUW members and others dressed in costume and portrayed five women in all eighteen public elementary schools in the community, and our Profiles of Women Project was born. The project eventually expanded to include intermediate schools and private schools, as well as school districts in other communities.

The monologues offered in this book have enhanced the educational experience of over 7,000 students annually. Through the short, five-minute living history presentations, students have had the opportunity to meet many notable women and have discovered the important contributions that women have made to society. Students have met remarkable women who overcame obstacles and reached their goals. In addition, girls have been provided with positive role models, and all students have been introduced to the wealth of women's history omitted from most history/social science textbooks.

Each year the success of our Profiles of Women Project surpasses all expectations. Students and teachers anxiously await the presentations each March. Presenters are cheered for their excellent portrayals and urged to come back.

Getting Started

The living history approach in this book brings history alive for elementary and intermediate students. It is particularly appropriate for these grades because it provides a multisensory experience, allowing students to actively see, hear, respond and question. It is also an appropriate way to introduce multicultural role models into the history/social science curriculum.

The monologues may be used in a variety of ways. They may be simplified or adapted as required for particular audiences. Use your imagination and be as creative as possible in their use.

Teachers, community volunteers, or students dress in costume and present the monologues to small groups, individual classrooms, or a school assembly. The monologues may be memorized or read aloud. One woman can be presented each day for one week, or several women may be presented at one time.

It is important to obtain prior approval from the superintendent, board of education and/or school principals in your area. The following samples are provided for your convenience in this book and may be easily revised to meet your particular situation or needs:
- Sample letters to school district, school principals and classroom presenters
- Sample media release and radio/TV spots

Also in this book are two items for distribution to teachers:
- Announcement Flyer
- Suggested Classroom Activities

For the presenters themselves, the following items are provided with each monologue:
- Reproducible full-page illustrations
- Suggestions for costumes and props
- Tips for presenters
- Suggested reading

There are numerous rewards for presenters. Months after the presentations, children often meet the presenters in the community and exclaim, "I know you! You're Amelia Earhart," or "Aren't you Sally Ride? I'm going to be an astronaut when I grow up." It is extremely gratifying to help students realize there are no limits to the goals they set or the careers they choose.

General Suggestions for Presenters

Being a presenter is a creative and gratifying experience. For a short time, you can be that famous woman you read about as a school girl or only recently discovered as an adult. To aid you in preparing for your performances, the following general suggestions were gathered from past presenters. Specific ideas unique to each woman are listed after each monologue. Add your imagination and ingenuity to make your presentation a memorable experience for both you and your audience.

Promoting Interest

Talk to the school librarian in advance about doing a Women's History Month bulletin board in the library and setting out books about the women who will be portrayed, as well as other notable women.

The school cafeteria is another good location for a Women's History Month bulletin board to promote discussion among the students. If time allows, change the board daily to highlight the woman of the day. Add news articles, photographs, copies of written material, etc.

Finding Costumes and Props

Costume shops can provide great ideas for costumes, but the best place to find materials for costumes and props is a thrift shop. It is also less expensive. Ask other presenters, friends, neighbors and relatives for help in acquiring items at little or no expense.

Don't be afraid to enhance your costume, to be dramatic and to stand out. You are there to make an impression and you definitely will. The students will remember you for years to come.

If you are portraying a person of another race, be sure to explain your character's ethnicity during the presentation and bring visual aids to help with your image. You might also explain at the outset of the presentation that there is now a law which prohibits a white person from painting his/her face another color to portray a person of another race. Ask the children to use their imaginations.

Rehearsing the Monologue

It is not really necessary to memorize the monologue. It is a good idea to know it very well so you can tell it in your own words, but there is nothing wrong with reading it aloud. Most of the presenters carry props that afford good hiding places for a condensed monologue or outline as suggested in the Tips for Presenters section at the end of each monologue.

Knowing Your Character

Keep in mind that the monologues are very condensed versions of one person's entire lifetime. Doing a little studying on your own prior to the presentation will give you a better insight into the person you are portraying and may provide answers to questions the students might ask. Also, the monologues may need to be updated with regard to the woman's present status, as well as tailored somewhat for different age groups. The better you know your part, the easier this is.

Scheduling Your Time

Starting with the lower grades (first and second), then going to the upper grades affords you the opportunity to "practice" in front of a more sympathetic audience. By the time you get to the upper grades, you should know your part pretty well. If you do kindergarten last, you will be so comfortable with the presentation that you can concentrate on the audience more, leaving out information they are obviously not interested in, and picking up on things that they are.

Respect the classroom time you have been allotted and answer limited questions. If the teacher is open to your staying longer, take into consideration your own time schedule for presentations in other classrooms. If time is limited, or if you do not feel comfortable answering questions, refer the students to the library and suggest that they find the answers and even more information.

Portraying Your Character

If possible ask the teacher to welcome you and explain the purpose of your visit when you arrive. Keep in mind that it is important for you to stay in character throughout your presentation. When answering a student's question, respond in the first person.

Having Confidence

Keep in mind that the children will be fascinated and appreciative of what you are doing. It would not occur to them that you may be feeling shy or nervous about standing in front of them. They will BELIEVE in you and the woman you are presenting.

ELIZABETH BLACKWELL

ELIZABETH BLACKWELL 1821-1910

I was told that no true lady would be able to stand the sights, smells and jokes of a medical school.

My name is Elizabeth Blackwell. It was in England, in 1821, that I was born. I was fortunate to have come from a family that believed in the equality of daughters and sons. I had nine brothers and sisters and we moved to the United States in 1832.

As I grew up, I was eager to be of real use in the world. One day I went to see a woman friend who was dying. She asked me to think about becoming a doctor and to try to find new ways of fighting disease. I loved my friend and thought hard about what she said.

At that time, however, a woman doctor was unheard of in the United States. My brothers were excited about the idea but others said it was unthinkable. I was told that no true lady would be able to stand the sights, smells and jokes of a medical school. Furthermore, there was the problem that women were not admitted to the schools that provided the necessary training. One doctor advised me to dress in men's clothing and attend some classes. That, he said, might give me some satisfaction; but of course, it would not give me a diploma. That suggestion made me very angry. I told him I was willing to go anywhere, even to hell, but I would go as myself!

I went to work as a music teacher in North Carolina to save money for medical school. The school principal I worked for had a doctor's degree and he agreed to let me read his medical books and help me study medicine. When I had saved up a sum of money, I went to Philadelphia where a Dr. Warrington allowed me to visit with his patients, attend his lectures and use his library. He helped me apply to all of the nation's medical schools. Some were polite, some were not, but the replies were all the same – "No."

Dr. Warrington then suggested that I apply to a few medical schools that were just starting. Finally, one school, Geneva College in New York, admitted me! I had no way of knowing that the head of the college had let his students decide themselves whether to

America's First Woman Physician

admit a woman student. They were in a playful mood that day, and as a joke, voted to admit me. I gradually won their respect, however, and went on to graduate in 1849 at the top of my class of 150 students.

It might seem that the worst was over. I was now free to practice medicine, but I realized that I needed more training because a woman doctor was going to have to be better than the best male physician in the world. I went to Paris for further study. Then something awful happened. While I was taking care of a baby with an eye disease, the infection went to one of my eyes. I became blind in that eye and had to give up my plans to study surgery.

When I returned to New York, I opened up my own office since no infirmaries (which were like hospitals) would hire me. Even after all I had been through, I found that people refused to believe that I was a capable doctor. No one had ever heard of a woman doctor. However, from time to time, through chance or an emergency, I did get patients.

My sister, Emily, had decided to become a doctor, too, and she and I rented a large, old-fashioned home where, in 1857, we opened the New York Infirmary for Women and Children. We expanded it eleven years later to include a medical college for women, with standards that were equal to those at men's colleges.

I lived to be 89 years old and in my later years, I went back to England where I lectured and wrote until I died. By sheer determination, I had become a good doctor but I had to spend most of my life proving it. In the process, though, I opened the doors for all the women doctors who came after me.

COSTUME/PROPS

Skirt and blouse

White lab coat with name badge

Stethoscope

Medical charts

TIPS FOR PRESENTERS:

Medical charts make great hiding places for the monologue.

Ask the class if anyone has ever been to a doctor who is a woman.

If you were able to obtain a stethoscope from Blackwell's time (circa 1850-1900), bring a modern one and show the differences.

SUGGESTED READING:

Baker, Rachel. *The First Woman Doctor: The Story of Elizabeth Blackwell, M.D.* Messner, 1944.

Brown, Jordan. *Elizabeth Blackwell.* Chelsea House Publishers, 1989.

Clapp, Patricia. *Dr. Elizabeth: A Biography of the First Woman Doctor.* Lothrop, Lee & Shepard Books, 1974.

Matthew, Scott. *The First Woman of Medicine: The Story of Elizabeth Blackwell.* Contemporary Perspectives, 1978.

Schleichert, Elizabeth. *The Life of Elizabeth Blackwell.* Twenty-First Century Books, 1991.

Wilson, Dorothy Clarke. *Lone Woman: The Story of Elizabeth Blackwell.* Little, 1970.

Amelia Earhart

AMELIA EARHART
1897-1937

My name is Amelia Earhart. I was born in Kansas in 1897. Instead of playing house or sewing doll clothes like other girls, my sister and cousins and I built a roller coaster from fence rails and wheels from old roller skates. We started from the roof of a shed and landed in the yard. It was just like flying!

I first became interested in real flying when I watched a World War I stunt pilot in Canada. Later, I decided not to continue college at Columbia University or go on to medical school. Instead, I went for my first ride in a small plane and begged my father for flying lessons. He refused because it cost $1,000, but I got a job at the telephone company and paid for flying lessons myself.

After only ten hours of instruction, I made my first solo flight. That means I went up by myself without my instructor. Then I set an altitude record of 14,000 feet. Flying in those days was not used for travel or for sending mail. It was considered dangerous, but I found it exciting.

I was able to show my courage by being a passenger on an airplane called "Friendship" that flew between the United States and England in 1928. I was the first woman to cross the Atlantic Ocean by air and I wrote a book about the trip called *20 Hrs. 40 Min.*

The next year I set the women's speed record by flying 181 miles per hour. In 1931, I wrote my second book, *The Fun of It,* and married George Putnam, the book's publisher. But I still continued my own way of life in the air.

In 1932, I flew across the Atlantic Ocean again, this time alone. Things went wrong on that trip. My altimeter failed, which meant I had to guess how high the plane was above the water. I hit a storm so I flew higher, but then had to come back down because ice was making my wings heavy. As I made my way through the fog, I noticed flames near my engine. I spotted some railroad tracks on the ground and followed them, hoping to find a city with an airport. Instead, I found a meadow and landed in Ireland next to

SOLO TRANSATLANTIC AVIATOR

the cows. The flight was considered a success and I had established a record crossing time of 13 hours and 30 minutes.

I then became the first woman to fly from Hawaii to the United States, the first to fly across the United States alone in both directions, the first to fly non-stop from Mexico City to New Jersey and the first woman to be awarded the Distinguished Flying Cross.

At age 39, I wanted to fly around the world at the equator – about 27,000 miles. My plane, the "Electra," had been given to me by Purdue University for research. Fred Noonan was my navigator and we started, in 1937, from Hawaii, flying westward. The "Electra" crashed before it was well in the air. It was repaired and two months later, we left from California and went eastward this time. We got to Florida, to Venezuela, across Africa, and then to New Guinea.

We planned to fly to Howland Island next and a ship in the ocean was going to help us find it with radio signals. But our gas was running low and we never found Howland Island. Thousands of people were involved in the biggest search in aviation history, but no trace of us or our plane has ever been found.

In a letter to my husband to be opened in case of death, I wrote, *"Hooray for the last grand adventure! I wish I had won, but it was worthwhile anyway."* My husband published *Last Flight*, a book based on my diary, which I had transmitted from the stopping places along the way on that final flight.

Other women have followed my path and have succeeded in aviation. They believed as I did that, *"Women must try to do things as men have tried. When they fail, then that failure must be but a challenge to others."*

COSTUME/PROPS

Jumpsuit or aviator jacket

Scarf

Aviator helmet and goggles

Picture or model of early airplane

Globe

Log book

TIPS FOR PRESENTERS:

The log book is a good hiding place for the monologue. Refer to it for dates, places and record times.

Use colored paper, string, or dot stickers on a globe to mark Earhart's last flight.

Mention or explain possible theories of what happened to Earhart. Suggest that students do their own research and see what they believe.

Explain what an altimeter is.

Mention that women have, indeed, gone into space. Tell about Sally Ride, the first American woman in space, or Judith Resnik, another woman astronaut who died in the shuttle explosion.

SUGGESTED READING:

Alcott, Sarah. *Young Amelia Earhart: A Dream to Fly.* Troll Associates, 1992.

DeLeeuw, Adele. *The Story of Amelia Earhart.* Grosset, 1955.

Earhart, Amelia. *The Fun of It.* Academy Chicago Publishers, 1977.

Earhart, Amelia. *Last Flight.* Crown Publishing Group, 1988.

Lovell, Mary S. *The Sound of Wings: The Life of Amelia Earhart.* St. Martin, 1989.

Rich, Doris L. *Amelia Earhart: A Biography.* Dell, 1989.

Sloate, Susan. *Challenging the Skies.* Fawcett, 1989.

GRACE MURRAY HOPPER

GRACE MURRAY HOPPER 1906-1992

Because of my

background in math,

the Navy assigned me

to work on the very

first computer called

the MARK I.

My name is Grace Murray Hopper, although my friends called me "Amazing Grace."

During the summer of 1985, I retired from the Navy as a Rear Admiral. At that time I was the oldest officer on active duty. Imagine that – no other man or woman in the Navy was as old as I was. Oh yes, at that time I was 80 years old!

My retirement and age were not the only reasons I was newsworthy. But before I tell you the main reason, let me tell you a little about myself.

I was born in 1906 in New York City. Right from the start I was curious about how things worked. Once when I was a child, I took apart seven clocks in our house. My mom was so angry that I spent the next several days in my room – alone.

I went to college at both Vassar and Yale. I earned a doctorate in math at Yale and joined the Naval Reserve in 1943. Joining the military was not so unusual for my family. Some of my relatives included a minuteman from the Revolutionary War, a captain from the Civil War and an admiral in the Navy .

Because of my background in math, the Navy assigned me to work on the very first computer called the MARK I. That was in 1944 and working with computers is how I became famous.

In 1945 when I was working with the MARK II computer, something went wrong. This computer, which filled an entire room, just wasn't working correctly. So I opened up the machine's doors and poked around the insides. What did I find? A moth! The moth had gotten stuck on part of the electrical wiring and was preventing the machine from doing its work properly. Once I removed it, everything clicked into place. And that is why we now say that if something is not working in a computer, it has a "bug" in it!

In 1949 I helped develop UNIVAC, which was the first computer used in business.

Pioneer Computer Scientist

I did not spend all my time just building the computers (the "hardware"). I also helped develop the programs which make them work (the "software"). As a matter of fact, I developed COBOL. COBOL is software which lets people tell a computer what to do using words instead of math symbols. This makes computers usable by everyone, not just mathematicians and scientists. I'll bet you use computers. How about the card catalog in the public library? That's a computer! And it works because of what I did.

Throughout my life I tried to help people understand that there is more than one way to solve a problem. I even had all my clocks run counterclockwise (or backwards) to show that there is even a different way to tell time!

After I retired from the Navy, I did not stop doing things. I worked at the Digital Equipment Corporation. I spoke to people in government and business, as well as students of all ages. My message was always the same – never stop learning. In fact, one of my favorite quotes was, *"A ship in port is safe. But that is not what ships are for. Be good ships. Sail out to sea and do new things."*

I died in 1992 at the age of 86. After hearing about my life, I hope now you can understand why my friends called me "Amazing Grace."

COSTUME/PROPS

Naval uniform (white blouse with gold epaulets, navy blue skirt)

Eyeglasses, gray wig

Small clock

Computer paper/disk/book

Moth (dead or alive) or picture of moth

Tape recording of "Anchors Aweigh"

TIPS FOR PRESENTERS:

This monologue can be enhanced by presenting it in a computer lab. Pictures of old style computers that occupied entire rooms make for good comparison with today's desktop models.

Begin by asking how many have ever heard the phrase "getting the bug out of a computer." What does it mean?

Computer paper or a disk is a good hiding place for the monologue or outline.

SUGGESTED READING:

Billings, Charlene W. *Grace Hopper: Navy Admiral and Computer Pioneer.* Enslow Publishers, 1989.

Mompoullan, Chantal. *Voices of America: Interviews with Eight American Women of Achievement.* U.S. Information Agency, 1984.

Slater, Robert. *Portraits in Silicon.* M.I.T. Press, 1987.

Wetzstein, Cheryl, and Forristal, Linda Joyce. "Grace Murray Hopper," *The World and I*, August, 1987, 198-205.

Zientara, Marguerite. "Captain Grace M. Hopper and the Genesis of Programming Languages," *The History of Computing, Part II.* 1981, 51-53.

BARBARA JORDAN

BARBARA JORDAN
1936 -

I am neither a black

politician nor a woman

politician. I'm just

a politician.

My name is Barbara Jordan. I am neither a black politician nor a woman politician. I'm just a politician.

I was born in 1936 in the State of Texas, and at that time in Texas black people were segregated (or separated) from white people. That meant because I was black, I could not attend school or use public parks with white children. I couldn't eat in their restaurants or sleep in their hotels and I had to sit in the back of the buses. My family and other blacks had to live in poor areas called ghettos.

I was lucky because my father was determined to help his three daughters achieve whatever they wanted but he didn't spoil us. He was very strict. We couldn't dance or play cards or even go to the movies. As a Baptist minister and a worker in a warehouse, he scraped together enough money to send all of us to college – in my case, all the way through law school in Boston, Massachusetts. To please him, as well as myself, I worked hard enough to make an A in every subject.

I wasn't pretty like my sisters. I was large, black and plain. I decided I wouldn't let how I looked stop me from being a success. Two things helped me: my deep, clear voice and my ability to use the English language well.

After I returned from Boston University, I had a law office in my parents' home. I spent my free time addressing envelopes for people who believed in the same things I did so that they could get elected to public office.

One night a speech was scheduled in a black church near where I lived. When the speaker became ill, I was asked to speak in his place. I was surprised by how excited the people were when I spoke. After that, I was asked to speak all the time.

TEXAS POLITICIAN

I eventually ran for public office and was elected to the Texas Legislature two times and then to the U.S. House of Representatives in Washington, D.C., three times.

I gained national attention during the Watergate investigations – a time when there was a question about whether our President or his staff was breaking the highest law of the land, the Constitution. I tried my best as a committee member. People liked what I said about the Constitution and quoted me everywhere. I said:

> *"My faith in the Constitution is whole, it is complete, it is total. I am not going to sit here and be an idle spectator in the diminution, the subversion, or the destruction of the Constitution."*

People were talking about my being Vice-President or even President of the United States some day. I was proud of that, but I realized that the time had not yet come for a black woman to be President. I decided not to return to Congress, but to dedicate the rest of my life to being the best college professor I could be.

I am now teaching at the University of Texas in Austin. My students know that I expect them to do well, but I am pleased to say that so many want my classes that a lottery system is used to see whom I will teach. At the end of each year, I give them a barbecue where I play my guitar and we all sing and have a good time.

I believe I may live to see a woman as President of the United States. I hope my students will live to see a black man or even a black woman become President.

COSTUME/PROPS

Conservative business suit

Briefcase

Texas map

Brightly colored button earrings

TIPS FOR PRESENTERS:

This character works well with a presenter confined to a wheelchair, such as Barbara Jordan is now.

A folder labeled "U.S Congressional Record" is a good monologue hiding place.

SUGGESTED READING:

Carpenter, Liz. "Barbara Jordan Talks About Ethics, Optimism, and Hard Choices in Government," *MS.* April, 1985, 75-76.

Haskins, James. *Barbara Jordan.* The Dial Press, 1977.

Jacobs, Linda. *Barbara Jordan: Keeping Faith.* EMC Corporation, 1978.

Keerdaja, E. and Henry, G. "Barbara Jordan College Teacher," *Newsweek*, August 3, 1981, 5+.

Roberts, Naurice. *Barbara Jordan: The Great Lady from Texas.* Children's Press, 1984.

Emma Lazarus

EMMA LAZARUS
1849-1887

If you visit New York, be

sure to read my words

on the base of the

Statue of Liberty.

You probably know that the Statue of Liberty is a huge figure of a woman holding high the torch of freedom. It stands on an island in New York Harbor. But do you know about the poem printed on its base? I wrote that famous poem. My name is Emma Lazarus.

My great-great-grandparents had sailed from Spain to settle in the United States. I was born in New York City in 1849, one of six children. My father was a successful sugar merchant and we lived in a large brownstone house in a beautiful neighborhood. I did not go to school, but tutors came to our house. They taught me the subjects that you learn at school and also to speak French, Italian and German. I loved to read English legends of King Arthur and myths about Greek gods so much that I gave my dolls storybook names from these books.

Then I began to write poetry. I enjoyed translating plays, stories and songs from French and German into English. In 1861, when I was eleven, the Civil War began. My uncles and cousins, dressed in the blue uniforms of the Union Army, left home; some would never return. The poems I wrote about the war spoke of "shadows of war that haunt" and "sunlight of the war's end."

When I was eighteen years old, my parents took me to a house party where I met Ralph Waldo Emerson, a very famous poet. We became friends and wrote letters to each other for many years. With his help, and the encouragement of other famous writers, I was able to improve my own verses. Often I wrote of truth and justice as a "perpetual lamp" or light. My first book, published in 1867, was a collection of poems and translations. Within a few years, I became a well-known writer.

Then something changed my life. As an American Jew, I was always treated well. But I now learned that in Europe, especially in Russia, millions of Jewish people were being driven from their homes and jobs. Many came to the United States hoping to begin a

STATUE OF LIBERTY POET

new life in a new land. They arrived by ship into New York Harbor. Ward Island was made into a kind of sleep-over camp and volunteers were needed to get food and health care for these homeless people. I visited Ward Island, and for the first time I saw what being poor really meant. The immigrants had nothing but the clothes they wore and they had nowhere to live. I gave money and food, but thought there was something more that I could do. I began to write stories and poems about them so that other Americans would want to help them. I became a crusader for freedom and hope.

Across the ocean in France, the people had recently overthrown Napoleon, their leader. They looked at democracy in the United States with great admiration and decided to build a statue as a gift to the American people in honor of our freedom. The sculptor called the statue "Liberty Enlightening the World." We call it "The Statue of Liberty." I was asked to write a poem for the dedication of the statue. That poem is called "The New Colossus." I thought about the people who came here with such hope and in my poem, the statue woman, named Liberty, says:

> *"Give me your tired, your poor,*
> *Your huddled masses yearning to breathe free,*
> *The wretched refuse of your teeming shore.*
> *Send these, the homeless, tempest-tossed to me.*
> *I lift my lamp beside the golden door!"*

If you visit New York, be sure to read my words on the base of the statue. I was only 38 years old when I died, but I was thankful that when a poet was needed to express what the United States meant to the people of the world, I was chosen.

TIPS FOR PRESENTERS:

The pad and pencil prop is a good hiding place for the monologue or outline.

Use other pieces of Lazarus's poetry on the bulletin board and, if time permits, read a favorite piece to the group.

SUGGESTED READING:

Angoff, Charles. *Emma Lazarus: Poet, Jewish Activist, Pioneer Zionist*. Jewish History, 1979.

Jacob, H. E. *The World of Emma Lazarus*. Schoken Books, 1949.

Lefer, Diane. *Emma Lazarus*. Chelsea House Publishers, 1988.

Levinson, Nancy Smiler. *I Lift My Lamp: Emma Lazarus and the Statue of Liberty*. E.P. Dutton, 1986.

Merriam, Eve. *Emma Lazarus, Woman without a Torch*. The Citadel Press, 1956.

ANNIE OAKLEY

ANNIE OAKLEY
1860-1926

I overcame great

hardships to learn a

skill and make a

success of it.

I was born in 1860 in a log cabin in the wilderness of Ohio. I was the sixth of eight children born to my parents, who were Quaker pioneers. They named me Phoebe Anne Mozee, but you probably know me by the name of Annie Oakley.

My father died when I was six, and we were very poor. I became a provider of meat for the family by making traps of cornstalks. I had always been fascinated by my father's rifle, and one day when I was 8, I sneaked it out of our house, took careful aim at a squirrel and *bang*, we had our supper! The kickback had given me a black eye and a broken nose, but that didn't stop me. After a little more practice, I became a crack shot.

When I was nine, my mother remarried, but we were still poor and I was sent to work at an orphanage. A farmer came to the orphanage and offered me a job helping his wife and taking care of their baby. Besides paying me fifty cents a week, he promised to send me to school, which I wanted to do more than anything. Two years later, because they treated me like a slave and had lied about sending me to school, I ran away and boarded a train for home.

Things had changed at home. My stepfather had died and my mother had remarried. We lived on a farm owned by her third husband, Mr. Shaw, but he owed a lot of money on it. I was determined to find a way to help my family. I had been hunting to put food on our table, but that wasn't enough. One day I took a string of game birds and a bundle of skins to town. By the end of the day, I had sold them all. Soon I was regularly supplying game to the hotels and restaurants in town and selling the skins to traders. I was making so much money that before long, my stepfather's farm was paid off.

When I was 15, Frank Butler's show came to town. He was a professional marksman and offered a prize of $100 to anyone who could outshoot him. Was he ever surprised when I challenged him! Well, I beat him! After the show, he took my family and me to

SHARPSHOOTER OF THE WILD WEST

dinner where he fell head over heels in love with me. I wasn't so sure about him, but I loved his poodle, George. I wrote letters to George, and Frank made sure that George wrote back. The next year we were married – Frank and I, that is!

We both went on the road with the show. I took the name "Annie Oakley" as my stage name. At age 24, I became the star of the show and Frank was my manager. The audiences loved the performances. These types of shows were as popular as football and baseball games are today. I would shoot an ash from a cigarette that Frank held in his mouth, split a playing card held edgewise and stand on the back of a galloping horse to shoot glass balls thrown in the air. I was a great athlete and a superb sharpshooter.

In 1884, we joined Buffalo Bill's Wild West Show and huge crowds came to see me perform. My clothes were copied by designers of outdoor fashions. If I appeared shooting from a bike, companies that made bikes would beg me to use theirs. I won many medals and trophies for my marksmanship and was as famous as today's rock stars and movie stars.

I had been in show business for 25 years when, after our last show of the season in 1901, we were in a terrible accident. Our train crashed and I was paralyzed. With determination, I learned to walk again and began performing in plays, which were not as hard on my body as the old shows. In 1912, I returned to the Wild West Show. Two years later, I retired.

Although Frank and I never had children, we supported eighteen orphan girls and paid for their education. I remembered the poverty of my childhood and the years at the orphanage. Just before my death in 1926, I melted down all my medals into one chunk of gold and gave the money to a children's home. I had overcome great hardships to learn a skill and make a success of it and I wanted to share the financial rewards of my success.

COSTUMES/PROPS

Western attire: mid-calf skirt, short boots, long-sleeved shirt, vest, cowgirl hat

Lariat (or other western gear)

Toy gun (check with principal)

TIPS FOR PRESENTERS:

The class may be interested in knowing that Annie Oakley was sometimes called "Little Sure Shot" because she was only five feet tall.

Annie Oakley can be compared to present-day sports stars. She was compensated by manufacturers when she used their products.

She also designed her own clothes because her style was unique at that time. Oakley designed and made the costume shown in the illustration. Ask how many students like to create their own wardrobes.

Explain "crack shot."

SUGGESTED READING:

Havighurst, Walter. *Annie Oakley of the Wild West*. University of Nebraska Press, 1992.

Kasper, Shirl. *Annie Oakley*. University of Oklahoma Press, 1992.

Levine, Ellen. *Ready, Aim, Fire! The Real Adventures of Annie Oakley*. Scholastic, 1989.

Quackenbush, Robert M. *Who's That Girl with the Gun?: A Story of Annie Oakley*. Prentice-Hall, 1989.

Sayers, Isabelle S. *Annie Oakley and Buffalo Bill's Wild West: One Hundred Two Illustrations*. Dover, 1981.

SANDRA DAY O'CONNOR

SANDRA DAY O'CONNOR 1930-

My name is Sandra Day O'Connor and I am a judge. In fact, I am the 102nd person to be appointed to the United States Supreme Court, the highest court of our country. I am the first woman ever appointed and when I was appointed, at the age of 51, I was the youngest Supreme Court Justice.

I was born in 1930. There was no hospital in the part of Arizona where we lived, so my parents had to travel hundreds of miles to Texas for my birth. Our house didn't even have electricity or running water. We lived on a 260 square mile cattle ranch we called the "Lazy B."

I went to school in Texas and I lived with my grandparents there but my summers were spent in Arizona on the ranch. Those were my happiest days – riding horses and roping steers. I learned to round up cattle and drive a truck and a tractor. I could fix windmills and repair fences. My friends and I played with dolls, but we knew what to do with screwdrivers and nails, too. Even now, I'm a pretty good shot with a rifle. I learned a lot living on the ranch. The great lesson my dad taught me was not to make excuses, not to ask for someone to bail you out, but simply to do the job yourself.

We liked to travel as a family – Mom, Dad, my sister, brother and I. Mostly we traveled to ranchers' meetings all over the western United States. On one visit to California, I decided to go to Stanford University. My Dad had planned to go to Stanford, but when Grandpa died, he had to run the ranch and never got to go. It was only natural for me to pick up on Dad's dream. I didn't even apply to any other colleges.

I have always loved to read, and I was very serious about my studies. I finished seven years of college and law school in only six, and I graduated with the highest honors.

While in law school, I worked on the college newspaper. There I met John Jay O'Connor. After my first date with him, I never dated anyone else. We've been married over forty years.

First Woman Supreme Court Justice

When I graduated from law school, I went looking for a job. I found out that law firms weren't ready to hire women. One firm wanted to hire me as a secretary. The others didn't want me at all, and here I had graduated third in my class out of 102 students, with highest honors, from one of the best law schools in the country!

Well, I kept trying and found a job as a county attorney in California. Later we moved to Arizona and I opened a neighborhood law office. That gave me the chance to try all kinds of law. It also gave me the time to spend with our first child, Scott. When Brian and Jay came along, I took five years off from practicing law to look after our growing family.

Then, in 1969, I became a State Senator in Arizona and was the first woman to hold office in any state senate in the country. I was a senator for five years. After that, I was elected to the County Superior Court. I ran my court strictly, but fairly. I had no patience with lawyers who were not ready to work. In 1979, I was appointed to the Arizona Supreme Court.

On September 26, 1981, President Ronald Reagan nominated me to the Supreme Court of the United States. Being the first woman justice of the Supreme Court is very important to me, but what is most important is that I be a good judge. We're all here, in part, to help others and to try to leave this place better than we found it. I have always thought that being a lawyer is one way to help others.

COSTUME/PROPS

Black robe

Gavel

Stanford University pennant

Copy of 1981 *Time* magazine cover

Lasso on end of rope

Screwdrivers and nails

Maps of Arizona and Texas

TIPS FOR PRESENTERS:

Have the teacher say "all rise" and wait for the students to stand before you enter the classroom, just like in a real courtroom.

Pictures of life on a ranch can enhance the idea that O'Connor's life has not always been in a courtroom. Write "ᗺ" on the board. Explain it is the brand from the "Lazy B" Ranch.

SUGGESTED READING:

Fox, Mary Virginia. *Justice Sandra Day O'Connor*. Enslow Publishers, 1983.

Greene, Carol. *Sandra Day O'Connor*. Children's Press, 1982.

Huber, Peter. *Sandra Day O'Connor*. Chelsea House Publishers, 1990.

Kohn, Howard. "Front and Center," *Los Angeles Times Magazine,* April 18, 1993, 57-62.

Woods, Harold and Woods, Geraldine. *Equal Justice: A Biography of Sandra Day O'Connor*. Dillon Press, 1985.

GEORGIA O'KEEFFE

GEORGIA O'KEEFFE 1887-1986

One of the jobs I held

was as a drawing

instructor to school

children in Texas. It

was there that I saw

the desert for the

first time and felt

inspired.

I am Georgia O'Keeffe. I was considered one of the great artists of my time and my career lasted over 70 years. I received many awards, including the Medal of Freedom and the National Medal of Arts. The reason for my success is very simple. It was not because I had a great gift; it was not just talent; it was because I learned to trust my inner feelings about my work and had the self-confidence to express "the world as I saw it" in my paintings. This took a lot of courage and a lot of very, very hard work.

I was born in Wisconsin in 1887, and was the second of seven children raised on my family's farm. I was strong and independent and never minded being alone. While other children were playing together, I would go off by myself and sit under a favorite tree in the meadow. I liked being different than my sisters; if they wore their hair in braids, I left mine straight, and I thought the ruffles and bows they wore were silly.

Walking to school each day with my brothers and sisters, I looked closely at the trees, the flowers and the animals. This fascination with nature never left me and has always been a part of my art.

My mother had a special love of music, art and literature. She read to us each evening. Often, she read adventure stories of the Wild West. The memory of these stories later lured me to the Southwest. She also had my sisters and me take drawing and painting lessons, and by the age of 12, I knew that I wanted to become an artist. Well, women in the early 1900's did not become artists but they could certainly teach art, so my family encouraged me to do just that.

When I was 20, I enrolled at the Art Students' League in New York where I found the city life, classes and student adventures exciting. My friends and I often visited the Alfred Stieglitz Gallery on Fifth Avenue. Stieglitz was a famous photographer who also presented new and unusual works of other artists.

A year later, family financial troubles forced me to give up my art education and I had to go to work to support myself. One of the

ARTIST

jobs I held was as a drawing instructor for school children in Texas. It was there that I saw the desert for the first time and felt inspired.

After four years, I returned to New York for further study. About this time, however, I was unhappy with everything I tried to create. I decided that my paintings were imitations reflecting the influence of my teachers. Where was Georgia O'Keeffe?

To find my own style, I put away my paintings, and using only charcoals, I worked until my fingers ached, sketching the visions and shapes in my mind. At last, I was drained of ideas and I showed my new work to my friend and fellow art student, Anita.

Secretly, she took them to Stieglitz. The fact that he liked them helped me to continue at a time when I was almost ready to give up. Once I had found my own style in the black and white charcoal drawings, I was able to use color even more powerfully than before. Stieglitz displayed my work for the first time in 1916, and I sold my first painting for $400.

Eventually, Stieglitz and I were married in 1924. I insisted on keeping my name and I became known simply as O'Keeffe.

After many years, I wanted to be in the desert again, so I spent the summer of 1929 in New Mexico. In the vast desert, I found sun-bleached animal bones and skulls and saw them as symbols of a long life and survival. When I returned to New York, I brought along a barrel of bones and enough visions of the desert to use throughout the year.

I continued to return to New Mexico often. After my husband's death in 1929, I moved there permanently. I enjoyed walking and climbing the hills and mountains. I collected things as I walked – sea shells that had turned to stone, beautiful white bones and rocks. I have used these things in my paintings.

In 1962, I was elected to the American Academy of Arts and Letters. I continued to paint and experiment with new forms of art, such as pottery, until I died in 1986 at the age of ninety-nine.

COSTUME/PROPS

Color xeroxed reproductions from books of O'Keeffe's paintings

Severe hair style (pulled back or with scarf)

Dressed simply, in black mostly

Little or no jewelry

Painter's smock, palette and brush

Vase of flowers

Cattle bones

United States map to show New York, Texas, Arizona, New Mexico

TIPS FOR PRESENTERS:

Ask how many students have visited a desert. What did they see there?

Are any of the students interested in becoming artists? What do they like to paint best?

Ask the students if they have ever walked along the beach or a path and picked up a shell or a rock that they thought was particularly beautiful.

SUGGESTED READING:

Eisler, Benita. *O'Keeffe and Stieglitz: An American Romance.* Viking Penguin, 1991.

Gherman, Beverly. *Georgia O'Keeffe: The Wideness and Wonder of Her World.* Atheneum, 1986.

Hogrefe, Jeffrey. *The Life of an American Legend.* Bantam, 1992.

Lisle, Laurie. *Portrait of an Artist: A Biography of Georgia O'Keeffe.* Seaview Books, 1988.

O'Keeffe, Georgia. *Georgia O'Keeffe.* Viking Books, 1976.

Beatrix Potter

BEATRIX POTTER 1866-1943

My neighbors knew me

only as Mrs. William

Heelis. They had no

idea that I was

Beatrix Potter,

creator of

Peter Rabbit.

I am Beatrix Potter. When I was a little girl, I loved animals. For many years, they were my only real friends. They were such a big part of my life that I wrote several books about them. In my books, they were like real people to me. I also liked doing drawings, called sketches, of them. Years later, my sketches were made into porcelain figurines and they were sold all over the world.

I grew up in London, England, over 100 years ago. My parents and I lived in a tall stone house and we had lots of servants. I wore pretty dresses with high necklines and dainty ruffles.

I had a rather lonely childhood. My parents loved me and were good to me, but they didn't play with me very much. I spent more time with the servants. I didn't get to play with other children very often and I didn't have any brothers or sisters until I was five years old. I spent a lot of time alone in my own room, on the third floor of our house. My friends were my pets, mostly live mice and rabbits, but I had a favorite doll, a wooden one named Topsy. I spent a lot of time reading and drawing but my animal friends kept me company. Oh, yes, I had one other special friend – my nanny whose name was McKenzie.

When I was five, my brother Bertram was born. Mother and Father decided that McKenzie was to take care of him and I was to have a governess who would also be my tutor. I liked having a new brother, but I was not happy about losing McKenzie to him.

Even so, my childhood seemed happier after Bert was born. We spent our summers in Scotland or in the Lake District where Bert and I explored the countryside. I loved the wildflowers, but animals were still my first love. I sketched the farm animals I saw grazing in the fields. Those summers gave me more ideas for writing, and I wrote more and more.

My governess thought I had talent in drawing and she told my father it would be good for me to take formal lessons. When I got a little older, I no longer needed a governess. However, we had

CREATOR OF PETER RABBIT

become such good friends that I never lost touch with her. I would write letters to her children in the form of picture letters. These picture letters were stories about animals. One of them was "Peter Rabbit," which I wrote in 1883 when I was twenty-seven years old.

Eight years later, I told some friends about these picture letters. They urged me to have these stories published but I was turned down by seven different publishers. So what did I do? In 1901 I published *The Tale of Peter Rabbit* myself, 250 copies of it. And guess what? One of the publishers who had turned me down before came to me and he offered to publish it. This was the beginning of my career as an author, one of the happiest times of my life. I earned enough money to buy myself a little cottage and I loved my new-found independence.

Then I met a nice man, a lawyer, named Mr. William Heelis. We were married and lived at Hilltop Farm. Our neighbors knew me only as Mrs. William Heelis. They had no idea that I was Beatrix Potter, creator of Peter Rabbit, Tom Kitten, Jemima Puddleduck, Squirrel Nutkin, Benjamin Bunny and others. I really didn't want them to know who I was. As an adult, I was a very private person, maybe because I had spent so much time alone in childhood.

To my new friends and neighbors, I was just a smart farmer and businesswoman. I could speak up boldly at cattle shows and sheep fairs. They saw me puttering about in my fields, where I usually carried a stick and had a lunch bag slung across my shoulders.

In 1943, I died a very happy woman. It is for all of you that I wrote my books. I wanted to share my animal friends with you. Some days if you are feeling bored or lonely, maybe they will put a smile on your face just like they did for me. Along with my beloved Hilltop Farm, I left ten farms, 15 cottages and 4000 acres of land to England's Historical Trust. If you ever visit the Lake District, you can visit Hilltop. You might even catch a glimpse of Peter Rabbit in my garden.

COSTUME/PROPS

Huge wicker basket full of heather or other wild flowers

Figurines or stuffed animals of Beatrix Potter characters

A few of Potter's books

Map of United Kingdom

Sketch book with pictures of Potter's characters

TIPS FOR PRESENTERS:

A monologue or outline can be hidden in the wicker basket, inside one of her books or inside the sketch book.

Sitting in a chair with Potter books and stuffed animals scattered around is a big hit for children.

Copy pages from Potter's books for the bulletin boards.

SUGGESTED READING:

Aldis, Dorothy. *Nothing is Impossible: The Story of Beatrix Potter*. Atheneum, 1969.

Frevert, P.D. *Beatrix Potter, Children's Storyteller*. Creative Education, 1981.

Lane, Margaret. *The Tales of Beatrix Potter*. Frederick Warne, 1985.

Mayer, Ann Margaret. *The Two Worlds of Beatrix Potter*. Creative Education, 1974.

Taylor, Judy. *Beatrix Potter: Artist, Storyteller, Countrywoman*. Frederick Warne, 1986.

SALLY RIDE

SALLY RIDE
1951-

I saw an ad in the school newspaper. NASA was searching for astronauts for the new space shuttle program. I applied and out of 8,900 applicants, I was one of the 35 chosen.

I was the first American woman in space. I was also, at age 32, the youngest American astronaut to circle the earth in a spacecraft. Maybe you know who I am. I'm Sally Ride.

I was born in 1951 in Los Angeles. From the time I was very young, I loved sports. I played baseball, football, soccer – and was as good as any of the neighborhood boys. I always played hard to make my team the best. When I was ten, I began taking tennis lessons and became so good that I received a scholarship to go to a private girls' high school. Physics, a science course, was my favorite subject, but I also loved to read.

When I began college, I continued to play tennis and became the 18th ranked junior player in the United States. One day, tennis star Billie Jean King watched me play in a match. Afterwards, she suggested that I quit school and become a professional tennis player. But after thinking about it, I decided to stay in college, and I graduated with two degrees – one in English and one in astrophysics.

When I was about to earn my doctorate from Stanford University, I saw an ad in the school newspaper. NASA (the National Aeronautics and Space Administration) was searching for astronauts for the new space shuttle program. I applied and out of 8,900 applicants, was one of the 35 chosen. Only six of those 35 chosen were women.

I then moved to Houston, Texas, for special training at the Johnson Space Center. In basic astronaut classes I learned all about the spacecraft's control switches, fire fighting, computer systems, parachute techniques, water survival and dealing with weightlessness. I also spent two years developing and working with a robot arm that would be used on future spacecrafts.

In 1982, I married Steven Hawley, another member of my astronaut group. That same year, I was thrilled to be chosen as one of the five crew members for the second flight of the space shuttle, *Challenger*. NASA's Director of Flight Operations said that I had been chosen because I was an intelligent problem solver and a good team player.

The day of the flight – June 18, 1983 – finally arrived! Over half a million people were at Cape Canaveral, Florida, to watch. *Four, three, two*

FIRST AMERICAN WOMAN IN SPACE

one, lift-off! The rocket engines roared as the shuttle leaped off the launch pad in a cloud of steam and a trail of fire. Inside, the ride was rough and loud. In only a few seconds, we zoomed past the clouds and suddenly, the ride became very smooth and quiet. We were traveling so fast that we went around the Earth nearly once every ninety minutes. That means we orbited Earth over sixteen times a day! It was weird because we couldn't even tell we were moving unless we looked out the window at Earth.

After the excitement of the lift-off, we settled down to work. During the seven days in space, we launched two satellites and retrieved one using the giant robot arm. We also ran lots of other scientific experiments. An exiciting part of being in space was being weightless. It felt wonderful to be able to float, but it was hard to move around. I started out "swimming" through the air, but before long, I discovered that I had to push off from one of the walls if I wanted to get across the room. Then, to stop moving, I had to take hold of something that was anchored in place. To sleep, we just strapped ourselves to the walls so we wouldn't bump into anything or into each other. We prepared our dried meals by squirting water into sealed plastic pouches to moisten the food. Because there was no gravity, we had to sip our drinks through straws from pouches.

Our flight touched down to a happy landing at Edwards Air Force Base in the California desert. Our mission was considered an outstanding success.

Since then, I've written a book and have spoken to many groups about my experience as an astronaut. I eventually left NASA and became a physics professor, first at Stanford University, then at the University of California at San Diego (UCSD), where I was appointed Director of the California Space Institute. This way, I continue to learn about space while teaching and encouraging young people to become scientists or astronauts.

When I was chosen for the Challenger's 1983 flight, reporters asked me a lot of silly questions because I was a woman. At one point, I told them that, *"It's too bad this society isn't further along and this is still such a big deal."*

COSTUME/PROPS

Flightsuit or blue jumpsuit

NASA patches

Helmet

Model or poster of space shuttle

TIPS FOR PRESENTERS

Ride described the launch of the space shuttle as "better than an E ticket ride." What did she mean? (Tickets to Disneyland were first sold in booklets which contained five types of tickets labeled A through E. The E-tickets were for the most thrilling rides, such as the Matterhorn.)

Mention that Ride's parents believed in giving their children the freedom to try out new things and ideas. They were always busy with things that interested them. Consequently, they ate whatever they wanted for meals whenever they wanted. Additionally, no one cared too much if the house was cluttered when everyone was busy. Discuss this type of life style.

SUGGESTED READING:

Behrens, June. *Sally Ride: An American First.* Children's Press, 1984.

Blacknall, Carolyn. *Sally Ride: America's First Woman in Space.* Dillon Press, 1984.

Hurwitz, Jane. *Sally Ride: Shooting for the Stars.* Fawcett Columbine, 1989.

O'Connor, Karen. *Sally Ride and the New Astronauts: Scientists in Space.* Watts, 1983.

Ride, Sally (with Okie, Susan). *To Space and Back.* Lothrop, Lee and Shepard Books, 1986.

Verheyden-Hilliard, Mary Ellen. *Scientist and Astronaut, Sally Ride.* Equity Institute, 1985.

ELEANOR ROOSEVELT

ELEANOR ROOSEVELT 1884-1962

I started a newspaper

column called "My Day."

I became a paid speaker

and traveled around the

country talking about

world peace and

human rights.

My name is Eleanor Roosevelt. I was born in 1884 in New York City to very wealthy parents, but I did not feel fortunate. You see, my mother was a beautiful woman, but I was very plain. I was tall and skinny and had teeth that stuck out in front. I did not smile often and I was very shy. I thought of myself as an ugly duckling. Because I was so shy, I had very few friends. My schooling was not in a classroom like yours. I had a tutor who lived in my home, so that means I did not have recess, team games or school vacations.

When I was ten, both my parents died, so my brother and I went to live with my grandmother. She was very strict. At 15, I went to stay at a private boarding school in England where the head-mistress (that's like a principal) took an interest in me. We went on vacations together and she taught me how to stand tall and proud and how to dress in clothes that actually made me look nice. I began to feel that the ugly duckling was becoming a swan.

Three years later, I returned to the United States and volun-teered my time in poor neighborhoods. You see, I had so much, I felt very sorry for the families, especially the children, who were homeless and hungry. At that time, children your age worked in "sweatshops," which were factories. They worked from early in the morning to late at night for a few pennies a day. The conditions were terrible and many died or were hurt by the large machines.

I was expected by my family to attend parties so I could meet a man to marry. There was a young man whom I enjoyed talking to, and his name was also Roosevelt – Franklin Delano Roosevelt. He was a distant cousin. Everyone was surprised that this handsome man spent so much time with me, but we were in love, and we were married when I was 20 years old.

Soon we had five children – a daughter and four sons. My husband spent his time with his law practice and politics. Although I was busy with my family, I wanted to do more, so I worked for the American Red Cross during World War I.

When my husband was 39, a terrible thing happened. He got

HUMANITARIAN AND UN DELEGATE

polio. That's a disease that paralyzes (or stiffens) the body, and he could not walk. Each day I helped him with his exercises, and finally he did walk again with braces on his legs and a cane. But he was always in pain.

In spite of his handicap, my husband became the 32nd President of the United States. I was his eyes and legs. I made speeches for him and visited many places he could not go. I spoke about changes in the laws, including those for the sweatshops the children worked in. At first, I was really afraid to speak before large groups, because when I got nervous, my voice sounded very high. However, I soon overcame my fear and became an accomplished public speaker.

During this time, the United States was going through the Great Depression. Millions of people were out of work. People wrote to me for advice and I, or my secretary, answered every letter. I started a newspaper column called "My Day." I became a paid speaker and traveled around the country talking about world peace and human rights.

In 1941, our country entered World War II. Many of our young men were wounded or killed. I visited them in hospitals here in the United States and in Europe. A few months after World War II ended, my husband died and the new President, Harry Truman, gave me a very important job. At age 61, I became the United States Representative to the newly formed United Nations. We were a group of countries who wanted world peace and freedom and better conditions for people living all over the world.

I stayed with the United Nations until I was 70. I became a great-grandmother and continued to write and lecture all over the world. Then in 1962, at the age of 78, I died. My funeral was attended by many important people, including President John F. Kennedy and two former presidents. I was buried next to my husband. Adlai Stevenson, a man who once ran for president, said of me, *"She would rather light a candle than curse the darkness."* I want to be remembered as a woman who loved her fellow people.

COSTUME/PROPS

Gray wig

Very little makeup or powder face

Picture of FDR

United Nations symbol or flag

White gloves, corsage, purse

Old-fashioned hat

Eyeglasses

TIPS FOR PRESENTERS:

Some of the following questions can be posed either during or after the presentation:

Why do you think my family never had my teeth fixed so they didn't stick out? We were very wealthy, you know. (Answer: there were no orthodontists then.)

How many of you are afraid of standing up in front of the class and giving a speech? I was. It can be very frightening, especially for someone like me who was so shy.

Who knows what the initials UN stand for? (United Nations) Do you know what they do? (Refer to a recent world situation where the UN was involved.)

SUGGESTED READING:

Faber, Doris. *Eleanor Roosevelt, First Lady of the World.* Viking Kestrel, 1985.

Goodsell, Jane. *Eleanor Roosevelt.* Crowell, 1970.

McAuley, Karen. *Eleanor Roosevelt.* Chelsea House Publishers, 1987.

Roosevelt, Elliott. *Eleanor Roosevelt with Love: A Centenary Remembrance.* E. P. Dutton, 1984.

Roosevelt, Eleanor. *The Autobiography of Eleanor Roosevelt.* Harper & Brothers Publishers, 1984.

Sacajawea

SACAJAWEA
1787-1889

My name is Sacajawea (Sak-uh-juh-wee'-uh), which means Bird Woman. I was the Shoshone Indian girl from Idaho who traveled with the Lewis and Clark Expedition. It was in 1805 and 1806 that we explored the wild lands of the West. As a result of the expedition, ten new states were mapped. Later, they became part of the whole United States.

I became famous because I was the only woman who traveled along with twenty-nine men where no one had ever gone before – over three thousand miles from the Missouri River to the Pacific Ocean and back – over many snow-covered mountains, sometimes without food – and all the time carrying my papoose, my son Pomp, on my back, as any Indian woman would do.

Before that, when I was 14 summers (or years) old, I was captured by the Minnetaree Indians, and I became their slave. Four years later I was sold to a French-Canadian fur trader named Charbonneau. Charbonneau knew some Indian languages, so he was asked to go along with Meriwether Lewis and William Clark to help make peace with the Indians. Because I was a woman with a baby, I would ordinarily have been left behind to wait. But I knew five Indian languages, including my native tongue, Shoshone, and Lewis and Clark felt that I would be important to them – especially since I could help them find the Shoshone Indians. The Shoshones had horses the white men could use to cross the mountains. I was excited about the trip! I would be able to see my people for the first time since I had been captured.

So, my husband Charbonneau, my papoose and I joined the famous Lewis and Clark Expedition. The idea for this trip was President Thomas Jefferson's. He felt it was important to learn more about the West, its geography, the life and languages of the Indians, and the fur trade.

I helped along the way to find roots and plants to eat. This kept us from starving when there were no animals to kill for food. Once, during a storm, our boat almost sank, but I saved many

GUIDE FOR LEWIS AND CLARK

important supplies and papers from being lost overboard. On the way back, I suggested a trail through the Rocky Mountains. That trail later became the route for the Northern Pacific Railway. There were council meetings with Indian chiefs and the white men, and I was allowed to sit with them. I helped them talk to each other and was present when they smoked the peace pipe. No Indian woman had done that before!

Many believed my greatest contribution to the expedition was my womanly presence. I made everyone feel better in difficult times, and a woman with a baby was a sign of peace to Indians everywhere.

When the trip was over, I did not receive any payment for my work, but my husband received $500. I didn't expect to be paid. However, Captain Clark was so grateful to me that he paid for the education of my son in St. Louis, Missouri.

In my later years, I returned to my people in the West. I showed them the medal President Jefferson had given me and I told them stories about the trip, which they told to their children and grandchildren. I started the Sun Dance among the Shoshones. This is a great three-day dance celebration. I learned it when I was a slave to the Minnetarees and, to this day, my people still do it.

I became known by all Indians as Chief Woman. In 1868, I was the only woman to speak at the signing of a treaty with white men. At age 70, I was considered quite lovely looking for an old woman and I could still ride horses as well as any man.

In 1889, I died at Fort Washakie, Wyoming. I was almost 100 years old. My people still talk about me and tell their children stories about me. They say, *"We honor her for her wonderful achievements for the white people – when they were on their way to the Big Waters."*

A river, a peak and a mountain pass have been named for me.

I, Sacajawea, sleep with my face toward the dawn – on the sunny side of the Rocky Mountains, at the Shoshone Reserve, looking over Wind River Valley.

COSTUME/PROPS

Indian attire (headband, fringed jacket, brownish tunic)

Braided hair

Map of Lewis & Clark expedition

Medal (received from President Jefferson)

Papoose on back in cradle board

Indian sign language examples

Beaded necklace

Peace pipe

Basket of Indian corn, edible plants, and beads

TIPS FOR PRESENTERS:

The basket with the Indian corn or other plants is a good hiding place for the monologue or notes.

If you have your own "papoose," bring him/her with you. If not, bring pictures of props to enhance this image. Young audiences have been very interested in the fact that she traveled with her baby on her back. Ask the students if they have ever traveled with their mother on a business trip.

Explain how beads were traded for information and that horses were used to traverse the mountains.

SUGGESTED READING:

Clark, Ella E. and Edmonds, Margot. *Sacagawea, of the Lewis and Clark Expedition.* University of California Press, 1979.

Gleiter, Jan and Thompson, Kathleen. *Sacagawea.* Raintree Steck-Vaughn Publishers, 1987.

Howard, Harold P. *Sacajawea.* University of Oklahoma Press, 1971.

Jassem, Kate. *Sacajawea: Wilderness Guide.* Troll Associates, 1979.

Waldo, Anne. *Sacajawea.* Avon, 1978.

Elizabeth Cady Stanton

ELIZABETH CADY STANTON 1815-1902

To suffer is to feel and put up with pain, and believe me, when it came to changing the laws of our states so that women could vote with men, the suffragettes experienced a lot of pain and suffering.

Whenever people talk about how women got the vote, or you read about women marching for the right to vote, my name, Elizabeth Cady Stanton, is right there with the other suffragettes. Those of us who worked hard for the right to vote were called suffragettes. The word "suffrage" means the right of voting.

It makes me think of the word "suffer." Who knows what "to suffer" means? That's right. To suffer is to feel and put up with pain, and believe me, when it came to changing the laws of our states so that women could vote along with men, the suffragettes experienced a lot of pain and suffering.

What we're really talking about here is equal rights. When you have to share a special dessert with others, you want to have your equal share. You probably really want a bigger piece, but in your heart, you know that's not fair. Well, that's what equal rights is about: wanting your share of life's opportunities and the right to share in decisions that affect your life. One of the ways we can share in decisions is by voting. It's probably hard to imagine a time when women were not allowed to vote. It would be like my asking you what game you would like to play today, and then saying only the boys could decide. Would that be fair or right? Of course not!

I was born in 1815. When I was eleven years old, my brother died and my father said, "Oh, my daughter, I wish you were a boy!" From that time on, I tried to prove that a daughter was just as good as a son. People like my father thought that women were not as smart or as important as men. Women were not allowed to vote in elections or go to the best schools. Some people even thought that women should not be allowed to ride bicycles!

As I grew up in Johnstown, New York, I wanted to go to the college my brother had attended, but it didn't accept women. Instead, I went to Troy Female Seminary. It was the first school in the United States to offer a college-level education to women. In the years after I graduated, I became interested in the anti-slavery movement and the temperance movement, which was concerned

WOMEN'S SUFFRAGE ACTIVIST

with the harmful effects of drinking alcohol. We're still working on that, aren't we?

In 1840, when I was 25 years old, I married Henry Brewster Stanton. He was a famous lecturer and believed in women's rights. We spent our honeymoon in England where Henry was a delegate to the World Anti-Slavery Conference. Women were not allowed to participate in the conference. They couldn't vote or express their opinions about what should be done. Can you imagine that?

Well, all the women who had come to this conference were very angry and made plans to organize a women's rights convention when we got back to the United States. The first convention was held in Seneca Falls, New York, in 1848. I wrote the Declaration of Sentiments. It was something like the Declaration of Independence, but it declared that all men <u>and</u> women were created equal. I demanded that women be granted the right to vote. The only way to bring about equality for women was by changing the laws that were unfair to them.

So, I began traveling across the country working for women's rights. I was the first woman allowed to speak in the New York State Senate. Although I was shy, my deep convictions (strong beliefs) caused the men in the Senate to give me a thundering applause.

I very much wanted to change public opinion about a woman's "place" and her abilities. I raised seven children, traveled, published articles in newspapers and magazines, and wrote books. All my writings and speeches had to do with trying to end the unequal treatment of women. I, along with many others, worked hard through the years for a woman's right to vote. Slowly, <u>very</u> slowly, public opinion began to change.

I died in 1902 at the age of 87 while writing a letter on a woman's right to vote. Eighteen years later, the 19th Amendment to our Constitution was ratified. In 1920 my hard work finally paid off when women in the United States were allowed to vote for the first time.

COSTUME/PROPS

Long white dress or skirt

Purple ribbon banner

"Right to Vote" sign or placard

Copy of 19th Amendment

TIPS FOR PRESENTERS:

Begin by asking if anyone knows what the 19th Amendment to the U.S. Constitution is. Encourage a discussion on what it would be like not to have a vote within your own group.

Ask the students if they know what the purpose of the temperance and anti-slavery movements were.

Mention that when the United States was founded, only white, male landowners were permitted to vote. The 15th Amendment (1870) gave African-American men the right to vote. Fifty years later, the 19th Amendment (1920) gave all women the right to vote.

SUGGESTED READING:

Banner, Lois W. *Elizabeth Cady Stanton: A Radical for Women's Rights.* Scott, Foresman and Co., 1987.

Clarke, Mary Stetson. *Bloomers and Ballots: Elizabeth Cady Stanton and Women's Rights.* Viking Press, 1972.

Cullen-DuPont, Kathryn. *Elizabeth Cady Stanton and Women's Liberty.* Enslow Publishers, 1989.

Griffith, Elisabeth. *In Her Own Right: The Life of Elizabeth Cady Stanton.* Oxford University Press, 1985.

Kendall, Martha E. *Elizabeth Cady Stanton.* Highland Publishing Group, 1987.

SOJOURNER TRUTH

SOJOURNER TRUTH
1797-1883

I decided to travel all

over the country telling

people the truth about

slavery. I called myself

Sojourner Truth because

I was traveling

and preaching

the truth.

I was born a slave in New York in 1797. My parents were owned by a Dutch family. On the day I was born, my master stopped by to see Ma-Ma Bets' new child. He approved of me and said, *"She'll make a sturdy worker."* I was named Isabelle, which was shortened later on to Belle. I never had a proper family name; that means I never had a last name. As a slave, I was not considered to "belong" to my mother or father. Like my parents, I belonged to my master, Colonel Hardenbergh.

We all became the property of his son, Charles, when he died. However, when Charles died, I was sold at an auction to the highest bidder.

My new master, John Neely, expected me to leap like a rabbit to obey his every command, even though I didn't understand his English language. I got the worst beating of my life from him. I wondered if it was right for him to do that. I then tried praying to God that He make my master good to me.

Still, things didn't get better and I prayed that my daddy might come back. He did, for a visit, and I begged him to get me a new master. My prayers were answered.

My new master had a preacher marry me to another slave named Thomas. I knew I could not marry Bob, a slave from another farm, because his master would take our children to be his slaves and I did not want to have my children separated from me.

Finally, in 1828, I became free under a New York law that banned (or outlawed) slavery. Because God had answered my prayers, and because I knew that the only way to change people's minds about slavery was to talk to them, face to face, I decided to travel all over the country, telling people the truth about slavery. I called myself Sojourner Truth because I was traveling and preaching the truth.

I became a great speaker, probably because when I was young, I practiced speaking whenever I was alone. Of my time, I'm

Abolitionist

probably the best known abolitionist (someone who wanted to abolish, or get rid of slavery). I was over six feet tall, had a deep voice, a quick sense of humor, and inspiring faith. Many people joined me in my fight to end slavery after they heard me speak.

I fought for the right of all people to become what they are capable of being. I believed that people best show their love for God by their love and concern for others. I wanted equal rights for everyone, including women.

One of my famous speeches was made in 1851 at the Women's Convention in Ohio. I said:

> *"That man over there says that women need to be helped into carriages and lifted over ditches and to have the best place everywhere. Nobody ever helps me into carriages or over puddles or gives me the best place... and ain't I a woman?*
>
> *Look at my arm! I have planted and gathered into the barns, and no man could help me... and ain't I a woman? I could work as much and eat as much as a man... when I could get it... and bare the lash as well... and ain't I a woman? I have borne 13 children, and seen most of them sold into slavery, and when I cried out with a mother's grief, none but Jesus heard me – and ain't I a woman?"*

In 1864, I visited President Lincoln in the White House. I stayed in Washington, D.C., to help find jobs and homes for slaves who had escaped from the South.

I am proud to say that our country honored me by having my likeness placed on a 22-cent postage stamp. If you ever see my stamp, I hope it will remind you of my belief that slavery had to be abolished.

COSTUME/PROPS

Long skirt with an apron

Scarf on head or simple white cap

Sojourner Truth 22-cent stamp

Shawl over shoulders

TIPS FOR PRESENTERS:

Ask if anyone knows what the "underground railroad" was used for and how it worked. (Refer to Harriet Tubman.)

Ask if anyone can imagine being bought and sold like a piece of property.

SUGGESTED READING:

Claflin, Edward Beecher. *Sojourner Truth and the Struggle for Freedom.* Barron, 1987.

Ferris, Jeri. *Walking the Road to Freedom: A Story about Sojourner Truth.* Carolrhoda Books, 1988.

Krass, Peter. *Sojourner Truth.* Chelsea House Publishers, 1988.

Ortiz, Victoria. *Sojourner Truth, A Self-Made Woman.* J.B. Lippincott, 1974.

Truth, Sojourner. *Narrative of Sojourner Truth.* Ayer, 1968.

BABE DIDRIKSON ZAHARIAS

BABE DIDRIKSON ZAHARIAS 1914-1956

Everyone called me

"Babe" because I hit

a ball just like

Babe Ruth.

My parents named me Mildred when I was born in 1914 in Texas. In school, my friends called me Millie – that is, until I began playing baseball. From that time on, everyone called me "Babe" because I hit a ball just like Babe Ruth. My name is Babe Didrikson Zaharias.

My mother, who was a fine ice skater and skier, and my father both encouraged all of us in sports. They even set up a gym in our backyard.

I was in second grade when I entered a marbles tournament at my school. In the finals I was playing against a sixth grade boy and won the tournament! I liked winning. I liked the glow it gave me, the praise, and the feeling of accomplishment.

In high school, I was a good student. Whatever I did, I wanted to do better than anyone else. I won first prize at the Texas State Fair for a dress I had made and I won a medal for typing 86 words a minute. I could also figure out math problems in my head quicker than most people could on paper.

Well, it was no different with sports. I wanted to run faster, jump farther, leap higher and play better than anyone else. To practice jumping hurdles, I jumped over hedges on my way home from school and asked one neighbor to trim his hedge because it was too high.

I could hit a hard ball that any of my brothers pitched and could roller skate circles around anyone on my street. I swam like a fish and dove like a seal. After playing tennis only three days, I entered a tournament and won.

After much hard work, I made the high school basketball team, even though I was small. I was the high scorer on the team, averaging 30 points per game. It was at this time of my life that I decided I wanted to be in the 1932 Olympics. Since there was no women's basketball competition in the Olympics then, I decided to train in track. At one meet, I ended up being an entire track team all by myself.

ALL-AMERICAN CHAMPION ATHLETE

My first event in the Olympics was the javelin throw. I set a new world record with my very first throw. It was in the 80-meter hurdle competition that I earned another first place, another world record, and another Gold Medal. Finally, in the high jump, the judges declared one of my jumps illegal. I felt I had been given a raw deal. I was not a good loser.

Even with the two Gold Medals, instead of the three I thought I deserved, I was the biggest star of the Olympic Games. That year, I was chosen "Woman Athlete of the Year" by the Associated Press.

Then I decided to play golf. I rarely ever lost. Very few men could hit a golf ball as far as I could. In one tournament, I was paired up with a professional wrestler named George Zaharias and suddenly I had a new interest. We were married in 1938. I thought seriously about what to do then. Should I stay home, be a home-maker and have children? But the children never came and I decided to keep doing what I really enjoyed – competing.

When World War II began, there were very few sports events to enter. So, I volunteered my time to the armed services. When the war was over, I got back to playing golf tournaments again. I set a record by winning 17 major golf tournaments in a row, and I was chosen "Woman Athlete of the Year" for the second time. I received that same award again four times in later years.

I then noticed a sharp pain in my left side. It must be a strained muscle, I thought, nothing to worry about. In 1951, we bought our own golf course in Florida, which meant more work for me. I enjoyed it, but the pain and swelling in my left side was bothering me. I suspected that I had cancer, but after an operation in 1953, I was back playing and winning in golf again. Then, I had more tests and more cancer was found. Eventually, I went into a coma and died in my sleep at age 45. President Eisenhower paid a tribute to me by saying, *"Every one of us feels sad that finally she had to lose."*

COSTUME/PROPS

Sweatpants or warm-ups

2 gold medals

Baseball cap with "BABE"

Tennis racquet

Golf club

Golf or track attire or a combination of sports attire

Basketball

TIPS FOR PRESENTERS:

Mention that the 1932 Olympics was held in Los Angeles just like the 1984 Olympics. Ask the students what they know about the Olympics.

Encourage the students to compare Zaharias's world records with those of today.

SUGGESTED READINGS:

Hahn, James and Hahn, Lynn. *Zaharias: The Sports Career of Mildred Didrikson Zaharias*. Macmillan Children's Book Group, 1981.

Knudson, R. Roazanne. *Babe Didrikson: Athlete of the Century*. Puffin Books, 1986.

Lynn, Elizabeth A. *Babe Didrikson Zaharias*. Chelsea House Publishers, 1989.

Smith, Beatrice S. *The Babe: Mildred Didrikson Zaharias*. Raintree Publishers, 1976.

Young de Grummond, Lena. *Babe Didrikson: Girl Athlete*. Bobbs-Merrill, 1963.

Zaharias, Babe Didrikson. *This Life I've Led: An Autobiography*. Barnes, 1955.

Appendix

SAMPLE LETTER TO SCHOOL DISTRICT

[Body of a letter to school superintendents, curriculum directors, school board members, etc. introducing the project and requesting approval to schedule classroom presentations. Send in January.]

In celebration of National Women's History Month in March, *(name of organization)* would like to provide students in your district with the opportunity to meet women from past or present history through a series of short, classroom "living history" presentations. For five consecutive days, volunteer presenters from *(name of organization)* will visit classrooms, in costume, portraying notable women from history. The presentations will be provided at no cost to the school district or to individual schools.

The women to be portrayed are: *(list of five women selected)*.

This Profiles of Women Project will give your students the opportunity to meet remarkable women who have overcome obstacles and reached their goals. They will discover the many important contributions women have made to our society. Girls will be provided with positive role models. Finally, all students will be introduced to the wealth of women's history often omitted from history/social science textbooks.

With your approval, we will contact the principals at all elementary and/or intermediate schools in your district to schedule the presentations. Please contact *(name and phone number of project coordinator)* if you have any questions.

SAMPLE LETTER TO SCHOOL PRINCIPALS

[Body of letter to school principals announcing the project and providing details about scheduling. Send as soon as possible after securing appropriate approval from superintendent, curriculum director and/or school board. Copies of illustrations of the five women to be portrayed, Suggested Classroom Activities, Suggested References, and Announcement Flyer for teachers can be included with this letter. Send copy to superintendent, director of curriculum, and/or school board as a follow-up to the letter introducing the project.]

In celebration of National Women's History Month, *(name of organization)* would like to provide your students the opportunity to meet women from past and present history through a series of five-minute, classroom "living history" presentations during the week of *(dates)*. For five consecutive days, we will provide volunteer presenters to visit your classrooms, in costume, portraying notable women from history. The presentations will be provided at no cost to your school, and will require no extra work for your teachers. We have obtained approval from *(appropriate information)* to schedule these presentations at your school.

The women to be portrayed are: *(list of five women selected)*.

The presenters assigned to your school will contact you directly no later than *(date — about one month before presentations)* to introduce themselves and to determine the best time during the day for the presentations to be made. The number of classes will determine the amount of time needed at your school. Each day during the week the classroom visits are made, the presenters will check in with you or your school secretary before they begin to see if there are any special considerations for that day. Please give your teachers a schedule for the week, and let them know that the presenters will wait to be acknowledged before beginning their presentations.

This Profiles of Women Project will give your students the opportunity to meet remarkable women who have overcome obstacles and reached their goals. They will discover the many important contributions women have made to our society. Girls will be provided with positive role models. Finally, all students will be introduced to the wealth of women's history often omitted from history/social science textbooks.

We thank you for your support of this project. Please contact *(name and phone number of project coordinator)* if you have any questions.

SAMPLE LETTER TO CLASSROOM PRESENTERS

[Body of confirmation letter to presenters regarding contacts with their assigned school. Send after obtaining appropriate school district approval, sending letters to principals and recruiting the volunteer presenters.]

Thank you for volunteering to portray (_____ *name of woman* _____) at (_____ *name of school* _____) on (_____ *date* _____) as part of this year's Profiles of Women Project.

Please follow these procedures when contacting and making the presentations at your assigned school:

1. By NO LATER than *(date referred to in letter to principals)*, please contact the principal or secretary at your school to introduce yourself and to determine the best time during the day for your presentations.

2. The day of the presentations, check in with the principal or secretary when you arrive at the school to see if there are any special considerations for that day.

3. When entering each classroom, wait for the teacher to acknowledge your presence before you begin your presentation.

Thank you for making time in your busy schedule to make women's history "come alive" for the students in our community. Please contact *(name and phone number of project coordinator)* if you have any questions.

SAMPLE MEDIA RELEASE

[Send 2 to 3 weeks in advance to local newspapers and/or media. The format given is correct, but the body of the release should be <u>double spaced</u>.*]*

NEWS RELEASE
FOR IMMEDIATE RELEASE
DATE: (*date the release is submitted*)
CONTACT: (*name and phone number of project coordinator*)
             (*name of organization*) VOLUNTEERS TO PROVIDE
             WOMEN'S HISTORY PORTRAYALS AT LOCAL SCHOOLS

Members of (*name of organization*) will make women's history presentations at local schools during the week of (*dates*) to celebrate National Women's History Month. Volunteers will visit classrooms, in costume, and portray five notable women from past or present history. The women who will be visiting classrooms are: (*list of five women to be portrayed*).

The purpose of this Profiles of Women Project, created in 1987 by the Thousand Oaks, California Branch, Inc. of the American Association of University Women (AAUW), is to introduce students to the many important contributions women have made to society and the wealth of women's history often omitted from history/social science textbooks.

SAMPLE RADIO/TV SPOTS

[Submit these fifteen second radio/TV spots, along with media release, to the person in charge of public service announcements at local radio and/or television stations. Follow up with a phone call to see if the station will tape volunteers reading the spots for broadcast during Women's History Month.]

Examples: • When I was 80 years old, I was the oldest officer in active duty in the Navy. I worked on the very first computer in 1944, and later helped develop COBOL, a computer language. I am Admiral Grace Hopper.
            • I'm neither a Black politician, nor a woman politician. I'm just a politician – a professional politician. I am Barbara Jordan.
            • The reason for my success was not just talent. It was because I learned to trust my inner feelings about my work. I painted enormous flowers and sun-bleached animal bones. I am Georgia O'Keeffe.

ANNOUNCEMENT FLYER

COMING SOON!

Profiles of Women Project

WHAT: Classroom "visits" by five notable women in history:
(each approximately 5 minutes in length with costumes and props)

- Emma Lazarus, Statue of Liberty Poet

- Sally Ride, First American Woman in Space

- Eleanor Roosevelt, Humanitarian and UN Delegate

- Sacajawea, Guide for Lewis & Clark

- Sojourner Truth, Abolitionist

WHY: To introduce students to the many important contributions women have made to society and to the wealth of women's history often left out of history/social science textbooks

WHO: American Association of University Women

WHEN: March 7 – 11, 1994

WHERE: Brookside Elementary School

TEACHERS:

Here is a chance to have National Women's History Month come alive in your classroom without any effort on your part.

If it is not convenient for a woman to visit your classroom on a particular day, please let your principal or school secretary know.

Sandy Hindy (123) 456-7890

Suggested Classroom Activities

1. Have the students make posters or collages celebrating Women's History Month for a classroom, cafeteria or school library display.

2. Have the students bring in pictures or articles about women from newspapers or magazines for a Women's History Month bulletin board in the classroom or elsewhere.

3. Assign a biography about a woman for the students' next book report.

4. Have the students research and write their own living history monologues, either about a woman in history, or their mother, grandmother, or other significant woman in their lives.

5. Schedule a filmstrip, movie, or video, etc. during Women's History Month to introduce students to the many contributions of women to society.

6. Integrate women's history throughout the curriculum. For example, read Emma Lazarus's poem during English or Language Arts, include Sally Ride during a discussion of space exploration in Science, have students draw Georgia O'Keeffe style pictures during Art, or try some of Babe Didrikson Zaharias's favorite sports during recess or P.E.

7. Play "What's My Line?" in the classroom with women in history as the "guests."

8. Prepare a crossword puzzle or word search for the students using the names or descriptions of contributions of women in history as clues.

9. Have students research and write brief "news" articles about women in history. Have them answer: Who, What, When, Where, Why and How? Assemble the articles into a classroom Women's History Month newspaper.

10. Have students research information about a particular woman in history. Then, have them take turns interviewing each other during a classroom "Women in the News" program.

11. Read aloud a biography of a woman during Women's History Month.

12. Duplicate the full-page illustrations found in *Profiles of Women, Past & Present* for classroom use.

13. Have the students write a letter to their favorite woman at the conclusion of the classroom presentations and send it to the woman who portrayed her.

14. Play "Hangwoman" using the names of famous women in history.

15. Have students write a speech they would give to nominate a famous woman to the Women's History Hall of Fame.

American Association of University Women

Suggested References

Reference Books:

Clark, Judith Freeman. *Almanac of American Women in the 20th Century*. Prentice Hall, 1987.

Handbook of American Women's History. Garland, 1990.

Statistical Handbook of Women in America. Oryx Press, 1991.

Women in Western European History: A select chronological, geographical, and topical bibliography from antiquity to the French Revolution. Greenwood Press, 1982.

Women's Studies: A Recommended Core Bibliography, 1980-1985. Libraries Unlimited, 1987.

Women's Studies Encyclopedia. Greenwood Press, 1989.

Histories:

Anderson, Bonnie S. and Judith P. Zinsser. *A History of Their Own: Women in Europe from Pre-history to the Present*. Harper and Row, 1988.

Bergmann, Barbara R. *Economic Emergence of Women*. Basic Books, 1988.

Davis, Flora. *Moving the Mountain: The Women's Movement in America Since 1960*. Simon & Schuster, 1991.

Evans, Sara M. *Born for Liberty: A History of Women in America*. Free Press, 1989.

Forster, Margaret. *Significant Sisters: The Grassroots of Active Feminism, 1839-1939*. Oxford, 1986.

Fox-Genovese, Elizabeth. *Within the Plantation Household: Black and White Women of the Old South*. University of Carolina Press, 1988.

Fraser, Antonia. *Weaker Vessel: Women's Lot in 17th Century England*. Random, 1985.

Giddings, Paula. *When and Where I Enter: The Impact of Black Women on Race and Sex in America*. Morrow, 1984.

Lerner, Gerda. *Creation of Patriarchy*. Oxford, 1986.

Miles, Rosalind. *Women's History of the World*. Harper and Row, 1990.

Norton Anthology of Literature by Women: The Tradition in English. Norton, 1985.

Stansell, Christine. *City of Women: Sex and Class in New York, 1789-1860*. Knopf, 1986.

Strasser, Susan. *Never Done: A History Of American Housework*. Pantheon, 1982.

Strong-Minded Women: And Other Lost Voices of 19th Century England. Pantheon, 1982.

Tentler, Leslie Woodcock. *Wage-Earning Women: Industrial Work and Family Life in the U.S., 1900-1930*. Oxford, 1979.

Wandersee, Winifred D. *On the Move: American Women in the 1970's*. G. K. Hall, 1988.

We Are Your Sisters: Black Women in the Nineteenth Century. Norton, 1984.

Women in Medieval Society. University of Pennsylvania, 1976.

Woolf, Virginia. *A Room of One's Own*. Harcourt Brace Jovanovich, 1929.

AAUW Information

The American Association of University Women (AAUW), founded in 1881, is the oldest and largest national organization working for education and equity for women and girls. Membership is open to all graduates holding a baccalaureate or higher degree from a regionally accredited college or university. In principle and in practice, AAUW values and seeks a diverse membership. There shall be no barriers to full participation in this organization on the basis of gender, race, creed, age, sexual orientation, national origin, or disability. For information about joining AAUW, call 1-800-821-4364.

A portion of the proceeds from sales of this book will be used to fund scholarships and fellowships through the AAUW Educational Foundation. This Foundation provides funds to advance education, research, and self-development for women, and to foster equity and positive societal change.